THE MOON

Small-but-Mighty Neighbor

MOON

Rocky, airless

Reflecting, waxing, waning

Phases, calendar, eclipses, ally

Orbiting, protecting, stabilizing

Small, mighty

SATELLITE

Hello, Earthlings! Universe here to show off more of my awesomeness. Today's topic:

Your moon!

Compared to my vast greatness, your moon is teeny-tiny. Miniscule!

But I know how important it is to you and your planet—it's Earth's cosmic ally.

Here we go again . . . Universe is bragging.

But it's about time Earth's moon gets the credit it deserves.

1

So, how did they become allies, you ask?
It's kind of a neat story.

I didn't pay enough attention to Earth when it was
young—I was too busy expanding. Then, all of a sudden . . . WHAM!

Oops.

A space object as big as the planet Mars slammed into Earth. There were rocks and debris floating all over the place.

But then . . .

That big space bully was named Theia. It ran right into little Earth!

Ouch.
Though I believe the correct term for Theia is "protoplanet."

. . . gravity pulled all that space junk together and **VOILA**, your moon formed.

Even after all this time, though, I'm sorry to say it's not a place where you'd want to live. It's one big, dusty, rocky desert. There's no air to breathe.

And watch out!

It rains space rocks! The moon's atmosphere is very thin and doesn't protect it the way Earth's atmosphere does.

The moon might not have much, but it does have your Earth. I've watched them grow up together, ever since the, um . . . *incident.*

But let's not talk about that.

As I was saying, they hang out. The moon orbits around and around your Earth at a steady pace, always keeping the same side facing you.

EARTH

Earth is lucky to have that moon—some planets don't have any moons at all.

There are more than 200 moons in your solar system. They come in all shapes and sizes. And while your moon is small, it is mighty.

It has been such a positive influence on Earth. **I'm so proud.**

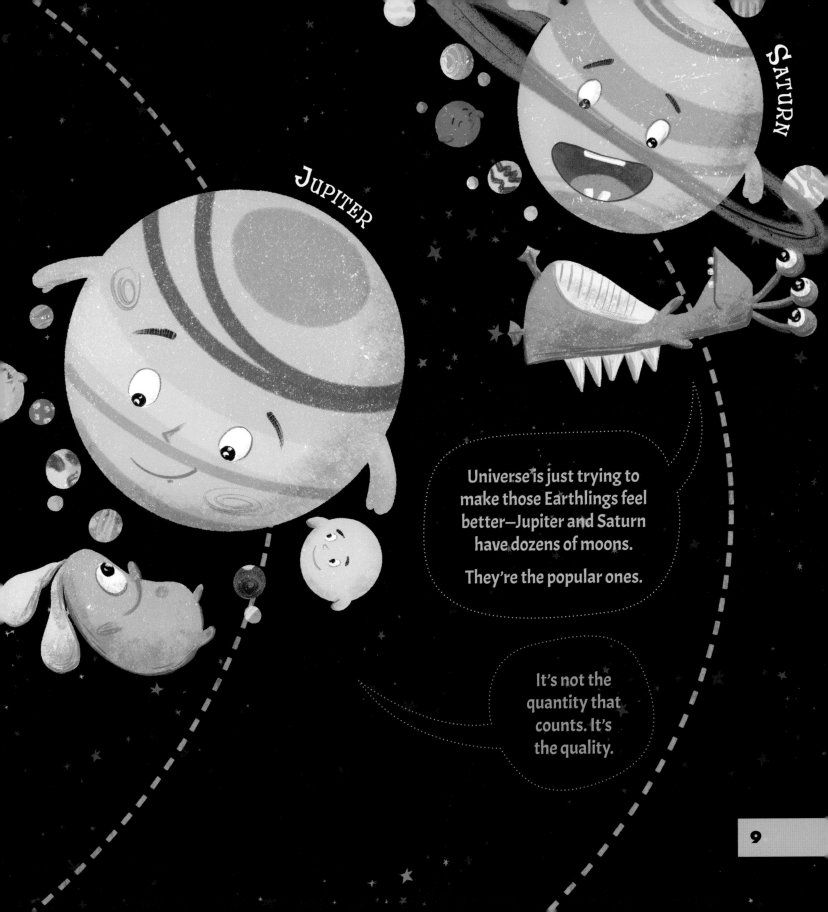

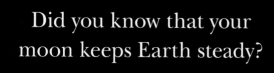

Did you know that your moon keeps Earth steady?

It does!

Its gravity prevents Earth from tilting too much on its axis.

Without the moon, your planet would be *very wobbly*.

All that wobbling would make for one crazy climate—imagine ice at the equator! I don't think there'd even be life on your planet without the moon.

Guess what else your moon does?

It keeps Earth from spinning too fast, like a toy top out of control.

I wonder if Earthlings and other life would be able to handle that. Because if Earth was spinning faster, you'd have faster winds. You'd also have stronger storms! And no one needs stronger storms.

The mighty moon also gives your planet tides. **No moon, no tides.**

Well, okay, there would be small tides because of the sun's gravity.

Booorrr-ing!

The moon's gravity is really what's responsible
for the regular high and low tides.

It's brilliant!

Next time you watch a tide come in or out,
just think—the moon is doing that!

That ocean is
always saying
hello to the moon.

How do
you know?

It's
always
waving!

You might think
the moon is shining up there,
like the sun and stars,
but it's not.

Really! It's reflecting.
That's right, it doesn't shine itself,
it reflects the light of the sun.

From Earth, you sometimes see ALL of the moon's
sunlit side. That's a big, round full moon. But have
you ever noticed that the shape of the moon changes?

17

Some nights, you might see a half moon.
Or just a sliver. Other times, you
can hardly see any moon at all.
That's called a new moon.

The moon isn't actually a
shapeshifter, though. It has to do
with how much of the moon's sunlit
side you can see from Earth.

WAXING GIBBOUS

FUL

FIRST QUARTER

WAXING CRESCENT

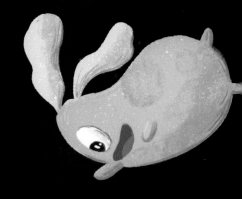

Sometimes, it looks like a yummy banana! Sometimes, like half a melon!

Yummmmmm.

It's the phases of the moon, not a buffet.

WANING GIBBOUS

THIRD QUARTER

WANING CRESCENT

Those phases of the moon go through a complete cycle once every month. That's how you Earthlings created the lunar calendar.

19

The phases of the moon affect animals' migration, communication, and mating, too.

Think of it as the social calendar for Earth's biodiversity.

The moon changes things on Earth in other ways as well.

And the little baby sea turtles use the moon to guide them to the ocean!

The moon tells coral when to spawn. It makes a plant in the Mediterranean weep. It helps dung beetles move in a straight line.

Sometimes, a lunar eclipse
happens during a full
moon. It's a grand show,
if I do say so myself.

What happens is
that the sun, Earth,
and moon line up
in that order.

And when they are in that nice, straight line, your planet casts a shadow on the moon.

Like magic,
POOF!
The moon seems
to disappear.

You can catch this show two or three times a year!

Do we need tickets?

23

You Earthlings **love**
all things moon. You even
tell stories about it.

Have you heard the tale of the man
in the moon? What about the story of
the cow jumping over the moon?

Twelve of you have even traveled up there to check it out.

You've collected moon rocks and sent dozens of robotic spacecraft up there!

Why don't we ever go to the moon?

Because the sunlit part is WAY too hot and the dark side is WAY too cold.

25

Your mighty little moon is pretty special. And even if you can't see the moon, Earth's loyal cosmic ally is always there.

Thank you, moon!

27

Phases of the Moon

To understand the phases of the moon, become an astronomer for a month!

Walking on the moon

WHAT YOU NEED

blank calendar for one month, pencil, colored pencils, circle stencil that fits in the calendar square (optional)

WHAT YOU DO

Put a circle in each box on the calendar. With an adult partner, go outside each night to look at the moon. Is it full? Do you see a crescent moon? A new moon? Color in the circle on your calendar to record the phase the moon is in. Observe and record the moon as it goes through the whole lunar cycle.

At the end of the month, look at your calendar. When the moon looked like it was getting fuller, it was waxing. In the phases when you could see less and less of the moon, it was waning. Is the moon waxing or waning now?

Ocean tide

How many days do you predict it will take for the moon to look full again? How long until the next new moon? How long was one full cycle?

28

Glossary

ally: a loyal friend who works together with you.

atmosphere: a blanket of gases around the earth.

axis: the imaginary line around which the earth rotates.

biodiversity: the great variety of life around the world.

climate: the weather patterns in an area during a long period of time.

crater: a large, bowl-shaped hole on a planet or moon.

crescent moon: when less than half of the moon is showing.

debris: the pieces left after something has been destroyed.

eclipse: when an object in space is blocked by another object, causing a shadow.

expand: to spread out and take up more space.

equator: an imaginary line around the earth, halfway between the North and South Poles.

gravity: a force that pulls all matter together, including planets, moons, and stars.

influence: to change something's behavior.

lunar: having to do with the moon.

mating: when living creatures come together to create new living creatures.

migration: the seasonal movement from one area to another.

miniscule: very small.

orbit: the path a planet travels around the sun or moon travels around a planet.

phases: the changing appearance of the moon during a month.

planet: a large body in space that orbits the sun and does not produce its own light. There are eight planets.

protoplanet: a small object in space, about the size of a moon.

reflect: to bounce back.

rotate: to turn around a fixed point.

satellite: an object that circles another object in space.

space rock: a comet, asteroid, or meteor made of ice, dust, and rock.

spawn: to produce eggs or young.

tide: the daily rise and fall of the ocean's water level near a shore.

universe: everything that exists, everywhere.

vast: huge.

waning: when the moon is getting smaller.

waxing: when the moon is getting bigger.

Full moon

Crescent moon

Earthrise from the moon

credit: NASA

29

SPARK SCIENTIFIC CURIOSITY WITH THIS PICTURE BOOK SCIENCE SET!

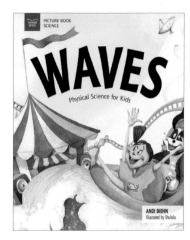

Check out more titles at www.nomadpress.net

Nomad Press

A division of Nomad Communications

10 9 8 7 6 5 4 3 2 1

This book was manufactured by CGB Printers,
North Mankato, Minnesota, United States
March 2021, Job #1018008

ISBN Softcover: 978-1-61930-988-3
ISBN Hardcover: 978-1-61930-985-2

Educational Consultant, Marla Conn

Questions regarding the ordering of this book should be addressed to
Nomad Press
2456 Christian St., White River Junction, VT 05001
www.nomadpress.net

Printed in the United States.